A Strong Ramadan Guide: Ramadan's Benefits Through Meditation and Spiritual Reflection

Mohammed B. Saeed

Table of Content

CHAPTER ONE

WHAT YOU SHOULD KNOW ABOUT RAMADAN

The ninth month of the Muslim calendar and the holiest month for fasting is known as Ramadan, or Ramadan in Arabic. The crescent moon's emergence marks both its beginning and conclusion. Ramadan can happen in any season during the course of a 33-year cycle because, unlike the Gregorian calendar, the Muslim calendar year begins 10–12 days earlier each year. According to Islamic tradition, God revealed the Qur'an to the Prophet Muhammad during Ramadan "as a guidance for the people" on the "Night of Power" (Laylat al-Qadr), which is honored on one of the last 10 nights of Ramadan, typically the 27th night. Ramadan is a time for reflection, al-t in the mosque, and reading from the Qur'an for Muslims. Those who celebrate the holy month with fasting, prayer, and sincere desire get God's pardon for their prior sins.

Yet, Ramadan is more of a time for Muslims to exercise self-control in accordance with awm (Arabic: "to refrain"), one of Islam's five pillars (the five basic tenets of the Muslim religion). SAwm is more broadly regarded as the prohibition against engaging in food, drink, sexual activity, and all other forms of immoral behavior between dawn and dark, including dirty or harsh thoughts, even though it is most frequently associated with the need to fast during Ramadan. Hence, just as eating and drinking can ruin a fast, so can misleading words, terrible behaviors, or bad intentions.

Muslims meet in their homes or mosques following the sunset prayer to break their fast with a meal known as ifr, which is frequently shared with friends and extended family. As was the practice of Muhammad, the ifr typically starts with dates, apricots, water, or sweetened milk. The tawar prayers are supplementary prayers that are offered at night and are best conducted in congregation at the mosque. Over the course of the month of Ramadan, the complete Qur'an may be recited at these prayers. In several nations with a majority of Muslims, daytime working hours are changed and occasionally shortened to make room for such evening worship. Eating and drinking are only permitted, according to the Qur'an, until the "white thread of light appears distinct from the dark thread of night at dawn." As a result, Muslims in some communities will ring bells or beat drums to alert people that it is time for the sur, or early morning meal.

By consuming food or liquids at the incorrect times, sawm might be invalidated; nevertheless, the lost day can be made up by fasting an additional day. Extra money should be set aside for anyone who becomes sick throughout the month or needs to travel. After Ramadan is over, alternate fasting days may be used. If required, fasting might be replaced by giving of one's time, doing good deeds, or feeding the hungry. Adults in good health and older kids fast during the day, from dawn to nightfall. The obligation to fast does not apply to children, elderly people, people who are weak or pregnant or nursing, people who are traveling a considerable distance, or anyone who have a mental illness.

One of the two major religious holidays in the Muslim calendar, Eid al-Fitr, also known as the "Feast of Fast-Breaking," marks the end of the Ramadan fast. Eid al-Adha, on the other hand, commemorates the completion of the hajj. the trip to Mecca that every Muslim is required to do at least once in their lifetime, provided they have the resources and the physical capacity to do so. Eid al-Fitr can be rather elaborate in some communities. Children wear new outfits, ladies dress in white, special pastries are cooked, gifts are exchanged, relatives' graves are visited, and people meet for meals with their families and to pray in mosques.

Eid al-Adha, also known as al-d al-Kabr ("Big Festival") in Turkey and as Kurban Bayram in Arabic, is the "Festival of Sacrifice." the second of two major holidays celebrated by Muslims, the other being Eid al-Fitr. Muslims around the world celebrate Eid al-Adha, which marks the completion of the hajj (pilgrimage) rituals in Min, Saudi Arabia, close to Mecca. It is distinguished from Eid al-Fitr by the performance of congregational prayer (al-t) at dawn on the first day. It starts on the tenth day of the last month of the Islamic calendar, Dhu al-Hijjah, and lasts for an additional three days (though the Muslim use of a lunar calendar means that it may occur during any season of the year). Families who can afford to sacrifice a sheep, goat, camel, or cow during the festival do so and then divide the flesh equally among themselves, friends, neighbors, and the underprivileged. Moreover, Eid al-Adha is a time for visiting with loved ones and sharing presents. Instead of Isaac, as in Judeo-Christian tradition, this event honors the ransom of the biblical patriarch Abraham's son Ishmael (Ishmael) with a ram.

Why do the dates of Ramadan change every year?

Muslims use a lunar calendar for religious purposes, one that is based on the moon's phases and has 12 months that total about 354 days. In comparison to the 365 days on the conventional Gregorian calendar, that is 11 days less. Hence, as comparison to the standard Gregorian calendar, the Islamic lunar calendar advances by around 11 days annually.

The starting day of Ramadan, the ninth month in the Islamic lunar calendar, therefore advances by approximately 11 days every year.

This has a significant impact on how individuals observe Ramadan year after year. Winter Ramadan is easier than summer Ramadan because the days are shorter, so you don't have to fast as long, and it's colder outside, so you don't have to worry as much about not being able to drink water all day since you're not perspiring as much.

Fasting might be difficult when Ramadan falls in the summer, though. Summertime temperatures in several Muslim nations of the Middle East and Africa can soar to levels normally only found in the lowest regions of hell.

Moreover, fasting can endure an average of 20 hours or longer in the summer in various Northern European nations, like Iceland, Norway, and Sweden (where there are Muslims, yeah). (And throughout the summer, the sun never truly sets in a few locations above the Arctic Circle. The closest Muslim nation or Mecca, Saudi Arabia, are the two options that Muslim religious authorities have ruled are acceptable under these situations.)

Okay, but why is there always confusion every year about exactly what day Ramadan starts on?

There is a reason that "Ramadan start date" always ranks among the top search terms. This is due to the fact that Muslims all across the world are unaware of the precise start date of Ramadan. If you Google it, you'll get a small disclaimer that states "Dates may vary" alongside Google's response:

It also has to do with conflicts over science, history, and tradition, as well as a little geopolitical competition.

The new moon marks the start of each new month in the Islamic calendar. Hence, Ramadan begins on the first day of the new moon. No problem, isn't it?

Wrong.

Here's a refresher of the moon phases in case it's been a while since you took astronomy in high school:

Because astronomical calculations were less accurate in Mohammed's day, in sixth-century Arabia, people relied on what they could see with the naked eye.

Muslims customarily waited to begin fasting until the faint crescent moon became apparent because the new moon isn't truly very visible in the night sky (as you can see above). Even a statement that the Prophet Mohammed is quoted as having said to wait to begin the fast until you see the crescent exists. Some believe that this is the reason behind the star and crescent. is the emblem of Islam, although the crescent has been used as a symbol for a very long time.)

This method was a little confusing, though, as various groups frequently began their fasts on different days, even within the same country, due to factors like clouds or the difficulty of seeing the moon in some regions. Rival parties would argue over who spotted the crescent first: the community, village, or even mosque inside the village may send its own man out to search for it.

Today, however, we don't need to wait for someone to notice a tiny crescent in the sky since we have accurate scientific equations that tell us precisely when the new moon begins. (In fact, the Oxford Dictionary of Islam states that one of the factors that motivated Muslim academics to study astronomy was the desire to ascertain the precise appearance of the crescent moon.)

Problem solved, then! Nonetheless, other Muslim scholars believe that we should continue to wait. Because that's what Mohammed said to do, and because that's how we've always done it, we'll wait until the faint crescent moon is visible in the night sky.

Others contend that Islam has a long history of using reason, knowledge, and science, and that if Mohammed were alive today, he would prefer using accurate scientific calculations to the alternative of sending the mosque member with the greatest vision outdoors to squint at the stars. Some others think that the globe should simply adhere to Saudi Arabia's official moon-sighting rules since that country is where Islam originated and where its holiest places are located, which would make things even more amusing.

Nevertheless, not everyone agrees it is a good concept, notably rival nations like Pakistan and Iran which object to presenting Saudi Arabia as the supreme authority in all matters relating to Islam.

All of this means that Muslims all throughout the world get to enjoy the lovely insanity of "moon-sighting combat" every year. There are memes about it because it's a Ramadan tradition that everyone knows:

Are there differences between how Sunni Muslims and Shia Muslims observe Ramadan?

Generally speaking, no. Muslims who are Sunni or Shia both fast throughout Ramadan. There are, however, a few small distinctions. For instance, Sunnis break their daily fast at sunset, when the sun is no longer visible on the horizon (but there is still light in the sky), whereas Shia wait until the sky is completely dark and the redness of the setting sun has completely disappeared.

In addition, Shia observe a different holiday during Ramadan than Sunnis do. Shia Muslims celebrate Ali ibn Abi Talib's sacrifice for three days, on the 19th, 20th, and 21st days of Ramadan. Ali was the cousin and son-in-law of The venerated fourth caliph of Sunni Islam and the first "valid" imam (head) of Shia Islam was Prophet Mohammed.

Ali was murdered during the bloody civil conflicts that broke out after Mohammed's passing about who should take charge of the Muslim society. While Ali was attending prayer on the 19th day of Ramadan in a mosque in Kufa, Iraq, an assassin from a band of rebels who disapproved of his leadership fatally stabbed him with a poisoned sword. Two days later, Ali perished.

In Shia Islam, Ali is a crucial person. Millions of Shia Muslims visit his tomb in adjacent Najaf, Iraq, which is the third holiest place in Shia Islam. Although they do not observe his passing or make a pilgrimage to his grave, Sunnis venerate Ali as one of the four "rightly instructed" caliphs who ruled after Mohammed.

WHAT IS RAMADAN?

For Muslims, Ramadan is one of the most sacred months of the year. Muslims fast from food and liquids during the daytime hours of Ramadan to remember the revelation of the Qur'an, to improve their relationship with God, and to develop self-control, thankfulness, and compassion for those who are less fortunate. Muslims devote a greater amount of time to devotional activities such as reading the Qur'an and offering special prayers throughout Ramadan, a month of intensive spiritual renewal. Fasting is not required for those who are unable to do so, such as those who are ill, young children, old, or nursing mothers.

When does Ramadan take place?

The Islamic calendar, which is based on a lunar year with 12 months and roughly 354 days in each, has 9 months, the ninth of which is Ramadan. Each lunar month advances by 11 days annually due to the lunar year being 11 days shorter than the solar year. The lunar months go through a full cycle and return to the same season every 33 solar years. The appearance of the new moon traditionally marks the beginning and conclusion of the month.

Muslims all across the world, including those in the United States, will start looking for the new crescent on March 22 or will observe a predetermined day based on astronomical calculations. The month-long Ramadan fast will start around March 23rd in 2023 and concludes about April 20.

CHAPTER TWO

The Length and Purpose of Fasting

Muslims observe a 29–30 day fast that lasts from dawn until dusk, which can range in length from 11–16 hours according on the season. For the duration of Ramadan, one must refrain from eating, drinking, and, if they are married, having sex during the day. Ramadan is a time for Muslims to train themselves both physically and spiritually by abstaining from any negative behaviors like backbiting, gossiping, lying, or arguing. Muslims look forward to Ramadan as a chance for introspection, spiritual development, and a way to develop moral excellence. Muslims invite one another to share a meal together and gather for prayers in the mosque during Ramadan, which is also a very social season.

Gaining more God-consciousness, or taqwa in Arabic, which refers to a condition of constant knowledge of God, is the ultimate purpose of fasting. A person should develop self-control, discipline, and a greater desire to do right and refrain from wrong as a result of this awareness. Muslims seek to read the complete Qur'an throughout Ramadan in remembrance of the book's revelation, which got underway during that month. Also recited during the special nightly prayers is the entirety of the Qur'an.

Who Fasts

Every Muslim who has reached puberty is required to observe the fast. Those who might find it difficult to fast are excluded from doing so. This includes anyone who is ill or on the go, women who are pregnant, breastfeeding, or menstruating, older persons who are too frail or sickly to fast, and anyone who are on their period. Except for people who are unable to fast due to advanced age or a severe disease, they should make up the fast later. Alternatively, they might provide food for a needy person for each day of fasting they skip.

What Happens if You Can't Fast?

Muslims who are exempt from fasting can make up any missed days at a later date in the year. If they are unable to make up the days, they must pay Fidya, a daily gift made in the name of charity that is used to buy food for people in need. Fidya typically costs less than £5 per day, though the cost varies from year to year depending on the cost of basic goods. For instance, if the Fidya is set at £5 and a Muslim missed seven days of fasting because of travel, they must pay £5 for each missed day, or £35 in total, to a Fidya charity.
When Ramadan is closer, you can check Fidya rates. If a Muslim must make a Fidya payment, they should do it before the fasting days they missed, but they must make the payment throughout Ramadan anyway.

What Happens if You Break the Fast?

There are two possibilities for breaking the fast: purposeful and accidental. Muslim who unintentionally consume alcohol or food between sunrise and sunset while fasting are still in compliance with the law and need not worry as long as they resume their fast as soon as they become aware of what they have done. One of the most fascinating Ramadan facts involves the indulgence of Sawm.

A Muslim is required to observe a 60-day supplementary fast if they purposefully break the Ramadan fast. They must pay Kaffarah if they are unable to fast for 60 days. In that it is a charitable contribution used to feed the hungry, Kaffarah is comparable to Fidya, albeit Kaffarah is much more than the sum of Fidya. If Fidya is set at £5 per day for seven days, and a Muslim purposely breaks their fast, they must pay a total of £300 (the cost of feeding 60 people) for each day. Since Kaffarah is based on Fidya, and Fidya fluctuates from year to year, Kaffarah also does.

To Muslim Assistance, a Muslim may provide Fidya and Kaffarah. We'll utilize it to provide food for the hungry and needy.

Children

Even though they are not compelled to fast until they reach puberty, it is normal for kids as young as seven to observe symbolic or limited fasts such fasting half days or on the weekends. This gently trains children and promotes inclusiveness throughout the month-long celebration. Children who are fasting for the first time the whole day or during their first Ramadan are frequently recognized in mosques.

Family Routines

A Muslim family typically gets up at around 5:00 a.m. before dawn and has suhur, a simple meal akin to breakfast. The family prays in the morning after breakfast before either going back to bed or starting the day, depending on the situation. People regularly nap in the late afternoon after work or school, especially during the lengthy summer months. After dusk, family members break the fast with a few dates and water, along with other light fare like soup, appetizers, or fruit depending on the culture. This is known as iftar, which literally translates to "breaking the fast." The family enjoys dinner after saying the evening prayers. welcoming visitors to a getaway In Ramadan, it's rather normal to fast or have iftar at someone else's home. Then, numerous families visit the mosque for the evening prayer and the taraweeh, a unique Ramadan prayer. Around 11:45 p.m., the family finish their prayers and head home. (These timings all change with the season, with less daylight hours in the winter and more daylight hours in the summer.)

Special Activities

Muslims can break their fast together during the daily community feasts that are hosted by several mosques. Students, the impoverished, and everyone who wants to take a break from cooking will benefit greatly from this service. On the weekends, a lot of mosques also hold a community dinner.

Most mosques hold taraweeh, or special Ramadan prayers, following the evening prayer. The prayer leader reads at least one-thirtyth of the Qur'an during taraweeh, ensuring that by the end of the month, the full Qur'an has been recited.

Muslims should be especially giving during Ramadan since fasting fosters compassion for the hungry Throughout Ramadan, numerous mosques organize food drives or charity fundraisers. At the end of the fasting day, many mosques also offer open homes where friends and neighbors of various religions are welcome to join them.

While thought to fall on one of the odd nights during the final 10 days of Ramadan, Lailat al-Qadr is most frequently observed on the 27th night of Ramadan. It is regarded as the most fortunate because it is thought that night in Ramadan was when the Qur'an was first revealed. While Muslims keep vigils in prayer, Qur'anic recitation, and meditation, mosques stay open all night.

Special Foods

The only truly traditional food practice related to Ramadan is breaking the fast with dates or water. It's interesting to note that dates, which are a concentrated source of energy and are simple to digest, are a good choice for this. For Ramadan, many Muslim-majority nations enjoy a wide array of special meals and sweets.

Eid ul-Fitr

Muslims celebrate one of their most important festivals, Eid ul-Fitr, also known as the "Festival of the Breaking of the Fast," at the conclusion of Ramadan. The holiday will fall on April 21st in

2023. Traditionally, parents, relatives, and friends give new clothes, cash, or gifts to children. The morning of Eid, a special prayer and sermon are held, followed by a community celebration, typically in a park or large hall. The celebrations include food, games, and gifts for the kids as friends and family spend the day talking, eating, and catching up with old friends. Eid Mubarak, which means "blessed holiday,"

What is a typical day like during Ramadan?

Muslims rise early in the morning during Ramadan to eat the first meal of the day, which must last until sunset. This entails consuming a lot of high-protein foods and staying hydrated up until morning, after which you are not allowed to eat or drink anything.

We offer the morning prayer at daybreak. Many people continue to sleep for a while because it's typically still early before awakening to prepare for the day (I certainly do).

Muslims are not supposed to skip school, work, or any other daily obligations because we are fasting. numerous Muslim nations, Yet, companies and schools could have fewer or no hours throughout the day. Despite being prohibited from eating or drinking throughout the day, Muslims often conduct their everyday lives as we would.

We break the day's fast with a short meal, really more of a snack, called an iftar (meaning "breakfast," before completing the evening prayer), when the call to prayer is finally made (or when the alarm on your phone's Muslim prayer app goes off). For the evening prayer and a unique prayer that is only offered during Ramadan, many people also visit the mosque.

Later on in the evening, a larger supper is typically served as a follow-up, which is frequently enjoyed with family and friends throughout the month in one another's homes.

After that, it's off to bed for a short nap before it's time to get up and begin again.

(Note: There are valid arguments in favor of breaking your fast with a little snack before offering the evening prayer and then eating a larger meal later. Muslims often move around throughout their prayers, including bending over, kneeling on the ground, standing up, etc. A formula for catastrophe is engaging in all that physical activity while stuffed full of food after 15 hours without a meal. Please believe me on this.)

The majority of Muslims, including myself, genuinely look forward to Ramadan and are a little sorry when it ends despite the hardship of fasting for an entire month. Knowing that tens of millions of your fellow Muslims are going through the same hunger pains, dry mouth, and lightheadedness as you are and that we are all in this together is just incredibly special.

So do you lose weight during Ramadan?

Some of you might be considering "Wow, what a fantastic approach to reduce weight! I'll give it a shot!" Ramadan is known for frequently causing weight gain, though. This is due to the fact that consuming heavy meals extremely early in the morning and very late at night, followed by a prolonged period of low activity verging on lethargy, can seriously harm your metabolism.

One meta-analysis of research studies on how Ramadan fasting affects body weight discovered that "The majority of the weight increases that occurred during Ramadan were reversed afterward, gradually reverting to their pre-Ramadan conditions. Although Ramadan presents a chance to reduce weight, sustained weight loss requires deliberate and consistent lifestyle changes."

You may drop a few pounds, just like with any other extreme diet plan, but until you genuinely adopt "structured and consistent lifestyle improvements," it's unlikely that you'll experience significant, long-lasting changes.

What can I do to be respectful of my Muslim friends during Ramadan?

Even if you are not Muslim, it is against the law in several Muslim nations to consume food and beverages in public during the daytime hours of Ramadan.

Of course, in the United States, where we have the right to freedom of religion (as well as freedom from it), this is not the case. Yet the majority of Muslims in America, including myself, don't anticipate a significant difference in the way that non-Muslims behave around us throughout Ramadan.

Although it was kind of my friends and coworkers to choose to fast alongside me in solidarity (or simply because it was "fun"), I never expect anyone to do this. (Furthermore, they often only survive around three days before deciding that camaraderie is overrated and that having a 15-hour thirst is not even really "fun.")

Having said that, there are several actions you can take—and avoid taking—to make life a little bit easier for friends or coworkers who also happen to be fasting for Ramadan. Maybe enjoy your wonderful, juicy cheeseburger in the office if you share a space with someone who is fastingInstead of leaving it at your desk where your poor, suffering Muslim coworkers will have to smell it and drool, place it in the break room (if they even have enough moisture left in their bodies to salivate at that point).

While it can be difficult for us to remember that we are fasting and is simple for us to carelessly accept and consume that Lay's potato chip you just offered us, try to keep in mind not to offer them a bite or a sip of what you are eating. But it's alright if you do. If you're doing it on purpose, in which case, what's wrong with you?, we won't be angry or outraged. Try to organize your dinner gathering for after sunset if you want to invite your Muslim friends so they have food. Although Muslims abstain from both alcohol and pork, we generally don't dislike it when it's nearby. Contrary to popular opinion, we just avoid eating pig; we are neither afraid of it or allergic to it. We're not vampires, and pork isn't garlic.) But, please inform us if item contains alcohol or pork so we don't unintentionally eat it.

You're welcome to simply say, "Happy Ramadan!" or "Happy Eid!" if you want to wish your Muslim friends or acquaintances a joyous Eid al-Fitr. That is not at all offensive. The customary salutations are "Ramadan/Eid kareem" (which means "have a generous Ramadan/Eid") or "Ramadan/Eid mubarak" (which means "have a wonderful Ramadan/Eid") if you want to show them that you tried to understand more about their religion.

Making your Muslim friends feel at ease and welcome can start with something as easy as memorizing one of those expressions and using it with a grin.

Charitable giving during Ramadan

Ramadan is seen to be the ideal time of year to engage in good deeds like charitable donations. It is believed that acts of generosity during Ramadan are multiplied many times over. Muslims donate millions of dollars to charities each year, making it the most popular month for paying Zakat (donating 2.5% of your wealth to charity).

CHAPTER THREE

How do Muslims Break their Fast in Ramadan?

Muslims eagerly anticipate breaking their fast when they hear the Maghrib Athan, "Allahu Akbar, Allahu Akbar," at the end of a long day of fasting. According to Surah Baqarah, Muslims must observe the fast.

The Qur'an was revealed throughout the month of Ramadan as instruction for humanity and as unmistakable signals that point to the right path and discriminate between good and bad. So, you must fast during the month if you witnessed it.

Al Baqarah 2:185

Many people are experiencing a time of physical and spiritual joy because they have avoided eating and drinking all day long, knowing that they will be rewarded.

As important as the fast itself is how a Muslim breaks their fast. While breaking the fast, it's crucial to do so properly and in accordance with the Prophet Muhammad's standards of behavior.

So how do we break our fast?

Breaking your fast at Sunset – Maghrib

At dusk, at the Maghrib prayer, is when the fast is broken during Ramadan. Since Allah explicitly commands in the Quran, "And eat and drink until the white thread of dawn becomes distinct to you from the black thread [of night]," you shouldn't put off breaking your fast. then finish the fast till evening [sunset]."
Al-Baqarah 2:187

According to this passage, fasting lasts from sunrise to dusk.

Breaking your fast with dates and water;

Muslims break their fast with dates and water because the Prophet Muhammad did so, which is known as the Sunnah.

This is in accordance with a Hadith that claims that the Prophet of Allah broke his fast with fresh dates before praying. He would break his fast with dried dates if there were none available, and if neither were available, he would sip some water.

Many Muslims still adhere to this ritual today, all around the world. That's why as soon as Ramadan starts, every grocery store pulls out their date baskets!

Being grateful

For Muslims, breaking the fast is a time of immense delight and comfort. It is a chance to thank Allah for His bounties and to think about those who are less fortunate. Muslims might also use this opportunity to hope for the prize Allah has given for those who observe fasts.

"Every good deed of the son of Adam would be multiplied twofold," stated the Prophet of Allah. If Allah wills, a good deed will be multiplied ten times up to seven hundred times. Except for fasting, which Allah says is for Him and that He will reward, this is true. For My sake, he forgoes both food and desire. The joys of breaking one's fast and meeting one's Lord are shared by the one who is fasting. Before Allah, the breath of a person who is fasting is preferable to the scent of musk.

Reciting the dua for breaking your fast

After breaking his fast, the Prophet of Allah would recite the following Dua as a way to thank Allah.

Insha'Allah, dhahab at-dhama' wa'b tallati al-'urooqu wa thabata al-ajr.

If Allah wills, the recompense is certain, the urge to drink has passed, and the arteries are moist.

This Dua can be attached to your refrigerator to serve as a daily reminder.

Breaking your fast with good company

Muslims are urged to share their meals with those who are less fortunate and to break their fast in the company of others.

"Whoever gives a fasting person food to break his fast with, then for him is the same reward as his (the fasting person's), without anything being deducted from the reward of the fasting person," said the Messenger of Allah.

Many people put this Sunnah into practice by hosting family and friends for iftar, going to neighborhood iftars at the mosque, or exchanging food with their neighbors. As a result of these neighborhood events, Ramadan is imbued with a wonderful and rewarding spirit of sisterhood and fraternity.